AF579981

SWIFT SPORT

SWIFT SPORT

CAR RACING UP CLOSE

Robert B. Jackson

Henry Z. Walck, Inc.
A Division of
DAVID McKAY COMPANY, INC.
New York

Most of these photographs by the author and his wife, Marcy, were taken at the United States Grand Prix, Watkins Glen, New York. They wish to thank Bob Kelly, Press Director of the Watkins Glen Grand Prix Corporation, for his many courtesies.

Library of Congress Cataloging in Publication Data

Jackson, Robert B
Swift sport.

SUMMARY: Describes the various aspects of automobile racing including the drivers, major races, components of a racing car and safety precautions.
1. Automobile racing–Juvenile literature.
[1. Automobile racing. 2. Automobiles, Racing]
I. Title.
GV1029.J257 796.7'2 77-014907
ISBN 0-8098-0013-6

10 9 8 7 6 5 4 3 2 1

Manufactured in the United States of America

Contents

The Drivers

The Cars

1

Swift Sport

Automobile road racing is a swift sport, with much exciting action. Important road races are held for several different classes of cars. Thousands of spectators go to each of these events. Most important of all are Grand Prix (pronounced *grahn pree)* races.

"Grand Prix" is French for "great prize." Grand Prix races are international contests that decide a World Champion Driver. Every two weeks or so, throughout most of the year, a Grand Prix is held in a different country.

Usually there are practice periods on Friday and Saturday of each race weekend. The race itself takes place on Sunday.

Many eager fans camp close to the race course for all three days in order to get the best viewing places.

In fact, some fans are already at the course early in the week, when the racing cars arrive on trailer trucks.

2

The Cars and Their Drivers

The top speed of a Grand Prix car can be almost two hundred miles an hour. When one thunders by, it often seems little more than a quick blur of color and blast of sound.

Grand Prix automobiles are by far the most advanced of all cars in design. Their powerful engines are located just behind the driver.

To save space and weight, the cockpit is very cramped. That little note on the steering wheel warns that new brake pads have been put on this car. The driver will have to be careful for a few practice laps until the brake pads adjust themselves, or "bed in."

At the front of this sleek car is a small wing. Without it, the car might lift its nose like an airplane on the long straights. Air pressure pushes down on the wing and forces the front wheels against the road.

Another wing at the back presses down on the rear wheels. As a result, the car will be faster through the twists and turns.

The rules require a red stoplight at the rear, just like those of family cars, to warn following drivers of sudden braking. (The supports hold up the rear wing, and the radiators cool both water and oil.)

Tires are very wide for the best possible grip on the road. In good weather, smooth "slicks" *(right)* are used. When it rains, tires with special grooved treads *(left)* are needed. The chalk marks show the owning team, the driver's initials, and the wheel location.

Drivers wear one-piece suits that can shield them against the first stages of a fire. They must also insert ear plugs because of the loud engine noise.

Further protection for the drivers comes from their long underwear, socks, and tight-fitting hoods. They are made of a flame-resistant cloth called Nomex. Drivers' shoes are lined with Nomex, too.

Each driver has his or her helmet painted in a different pattern of colors. This makes it easy for fans to spot their favorites as they flash past. The clear visor snaps closed for racing.

Drivers also wear Nomex gloves. Dressed in all this warm clothing and wedged close to the hot engine, drivers can become very uncomfortable.

3

Practice

The cars are taken completely apart before each race. They are carefully examined and then rebuilt. Teams are always searching for more speed, so possible improvements are made at the same time.

Finally, all is ready. Each lap of each car will be officially timed on both days of practice. Then the cars will start the race according to their best practice times. The fastest car will be at the front, and the slowest at the rear.

During practice periods, drivers try to find the fastest route through each of the many turns. They must also learn where to brake and where to shift gears in dozens of locations. They keep looking for lower lap times.

Every few laps, the drivers come in to the pits and report. Team managers then consider changes in mechanical settings that might make the cars faster.

After each change, the driver rushes out of the pit lane to strive for a quicker lap.

But not every idea works, and more hurried conferences may be needed.

Tire experts regularly check the temperature of the treads. In this way they can tell how well the tires are sticking to the road. Further adjustments of the car may be necessary to increase the tire "bite."

Teams keep an exact record of their own lap times to know how well they are doing. They also time the cars of their chief rivals. Lap times of the best cars and drivers generally differ by only the smallest fractions of a second.

This improvised bulletin board is being kept on the wall of one of the pits. The "X" shows that Ronnie Peterson has turned the fastest practice lap so far—1 minute, 57.7 seconds.

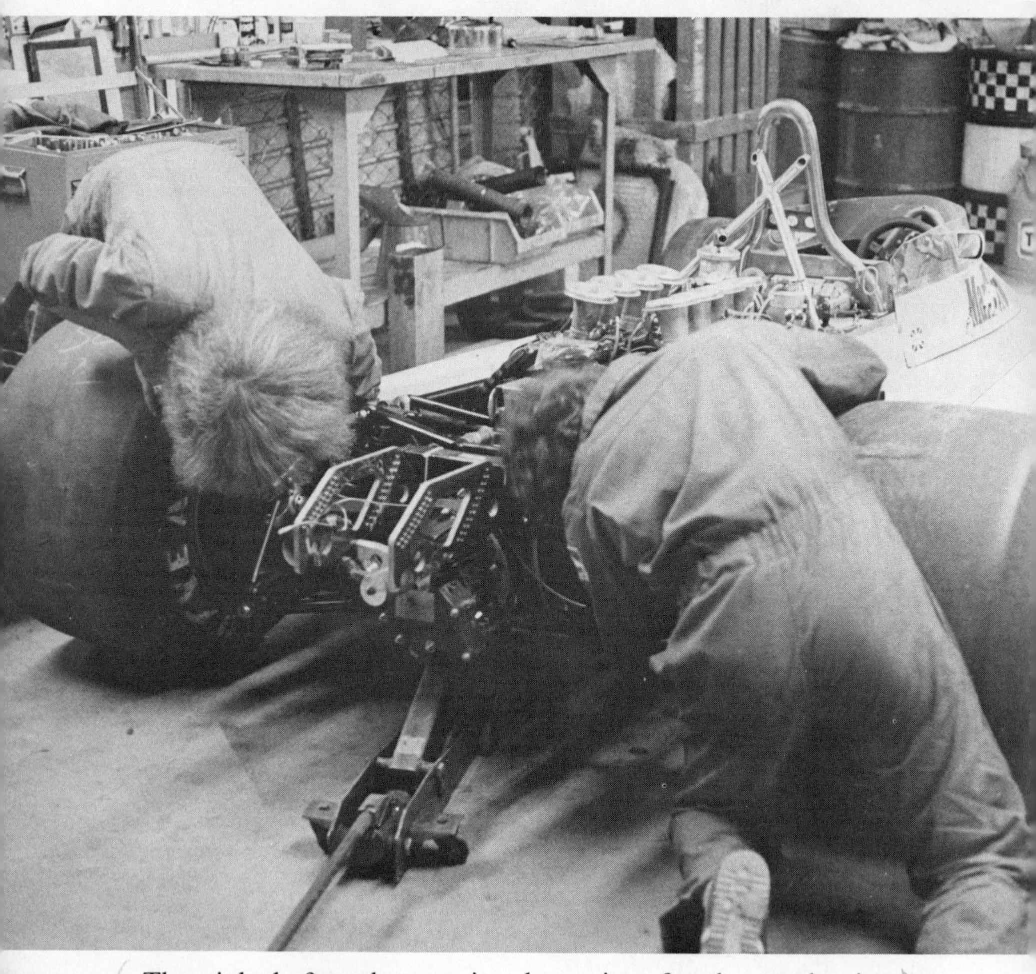

The night before the race is a busy time for the mechanics. They often replace engines, and there may be accident damage to repair. In any case, they must clean and inspect every part of the car.

4

Before the Race

Early on the morning of the race, many fans walk the course to get a closer look at it. Most road courses are several miles around.

After the course has been closed to spectators, the corner workers drive out to their positions. Dressed in white to be seen easily, a group is located close to the road at each turn. They exchange reports with race officials by telephone or radio.

One of the corner workers' biggest jobs is passing information along to the drivers. They do this by waving large colored flags. A green flag means "No trouble ahead," for instance. A yellow flag signals caution. Here a striped flag warns that oil has leaked onto the road.

With excitement increasing all the while, a preliminary event is often held. This one is for historic racing cars.

The drivers for the big race are eventually paraded in open cars, while cheers and applause follow them around the circuit.

By now, the fences surrounding the course are lined with spectators. The large grandstands are also filled, but these fans have climbed to an unusual lookout.

In the pits, mechanics have already neatly laid out their tools. They do not want to waste time looking for a wrench that is needed in a hurry.

Overhead, a large blimp begins to drift around the circuit. It often carries a television camera.

The drivers become quiet and adjust their helmets, perhaps taking a little longer than necessary in order to keep busy.

At last the cars are slowly pushed out to their places on the starting "grid." Each team is hoping to do as well as they possibly can.

The drivers are strapped into their cockpits. Then a cannon is fired to warn everyone else off the grid. The most exciting moment of the race is at hand.

5

Wheel to Wheel

Nowadays, a race is sometimes started by the blink of a green light, but the old-fashioned wave of a green flag is more dramatic.

The cars spring forward in an explosion of noise and dust, their drivers fighting for position through the first turn.

When the first lap has been completed, most of the colorful cars are still strung out nose to tail.

The race is usually about two hundred miles long, and the drivers push their cars to the limit from start to finish.

At such high speeds, a car may go off course at any time. This car is sliding in the grass, its driver having lost control in a turn.

To stop such cars, a series of “catch fences” are located at the most difficult parts of the course. They are built to sag inward and gradually trap an automobile.

As the cars roar past the pits, crews hold signal boards for their drivers. The boards show such important numbers as overall position and time for the last lap. A driver may also want to know how far ahead—or behind—a close competitor is running.

Some teams have recently replaced pit boards with two-way radios. The driver and team manager can talk to each other throughout the race.

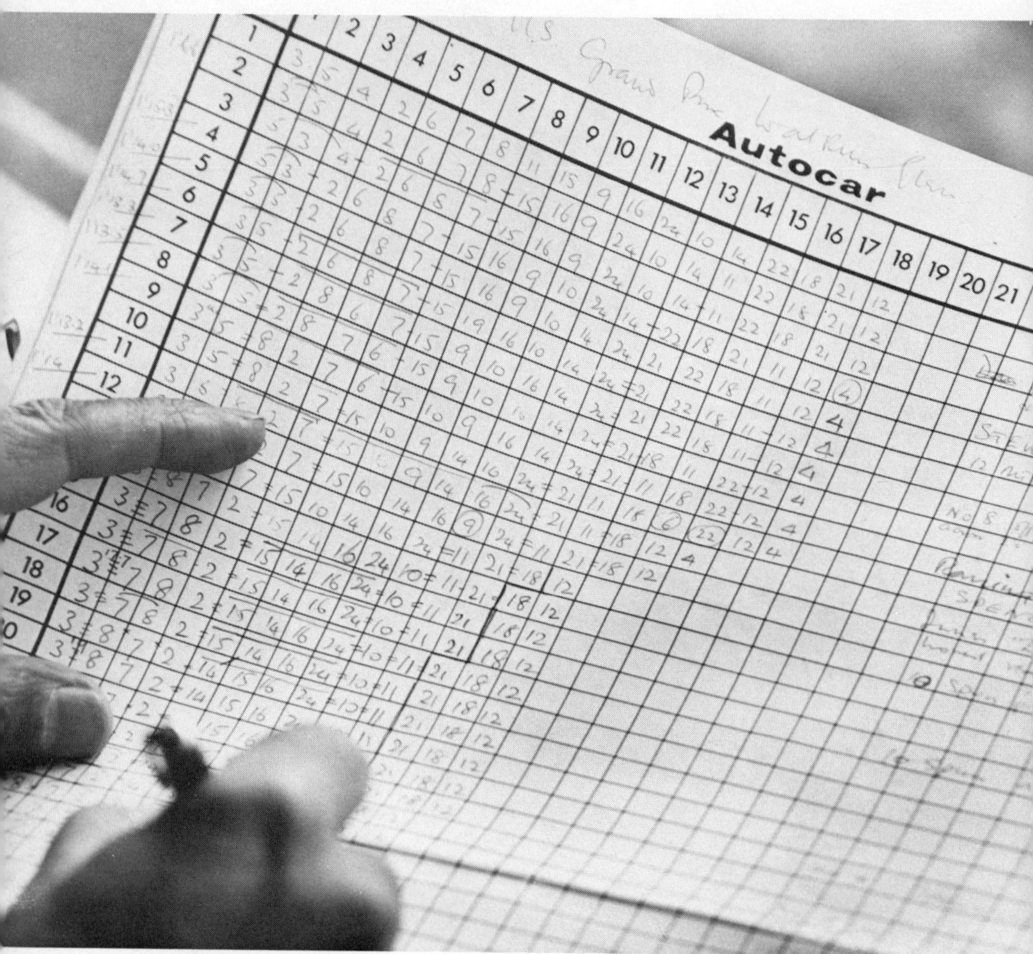

Teams and reporters keep track of the race by rapidly writing the car numbers in race order for each lap. Making a lap chart like this is not as easy as it looks, because the cars streak past quickly and in bunches.

6

At the Finish

Ordinarily, a car stopping at its pit for mechanical repair will be left far behind. However, a sudden rainstorm can bring everyone in to the pits for a change of tires. Such pit stops can scramble the standings.

Back out on the course, the difficult test continues. The racers sweep through curves and hurtle down straights, at times only inches apart.

The lead car is almost touching the curbing in taking the shortest way around. A skilled driver will follow the same precise "line" through a turn, lap after lap.

Drivers are tiring from the strain at this point, but they dare not let their attention wander. The leaders are also hoping that their cars will not break down during the last few laps.

At the climax of the long weekend, the winner is first to take the checkered flag. The engines then fall silent, and spectators start packing for the long trip home.

Before they leave, though, many fans watch the victory ceremony and cheer the happy winner.